PowerKids Readers:
Nature Books™

Rain

Kristin Ward

The Rosen Publishing Group's
PowerKids Press™
New York

1

For Thomas and Mak, with love.

Published in 2000 by The Rosen Publishing Group, Inc.
29 East 21st Street, New York, NY 10010

First Edition

Book design: Michael de Guzman

Photo Credits: p. 1 © Peter Gridley/FPG International and CORBIS/Jacqui Hurst; p. 5 © Kenneth Garrett/FPG International; p. 7 © Willie Holdman/International Stock; p. 9 © Arthur Tilley/FPG International; p. 11 © Dennie Cody/FPG International Stock; p. 13 © Randy Masser/International Stock; p. 15 © Bob Firth/International Stock; p. 17 © Maratea/International Stock; p. 19 © Wayne Aldridge/International Stock; p. 21 CORBIS/Bruce Burkhardt.

Ward, Kristin.
    Rain / by Kristin Ward.
        p. cm. — (Nature books)
Includes index.
Summary: Describes what rain is and how it helps plants animals, and people.
ISBN 0-8239-5531-1
1. Rain—Juvenile literature. 2. Weather—Juvenile literature. [1. Rain. 2. Weather.] I. Title. II. Series: Nature books (New York, N.Y.)
SB481.3.W27 1999
790—dc21   98-53866
                                                                CIP
                                                                 AC

Manufactured in the United States of America

Contents

Rain falls from clouds in the sky.

5

Rain is made up of tiny drops of water. We call them raindrops.

In a drizzle, just a little rain falls from the sky.

In a storm, a lot of rain falls from the sky.

11

When rain falls, it helps flowers grow.

13

Rain helps the grass stay green.

15

Rain gives people and animals water to drink.

Rain helps keep lakes full.

19

Rain even makes puddles
that are fun to jump in!

Words to Know

CLOUD   FLOWER   GRASS

LAKE   PUDDLE   RAIN

RAINDROP

Here are more books to read about rain:
Down Comes the Rain (Let's-Read-And-Find-Out-Science)
by James Graham Hale (illustrator), Franklyn Mansfield Branley
HarperCollins Juvenile Books

From Ice to Rain
by Marlene Reidel, Ali Mitgutsch, Annegert Fuchshuber
Carolrhoda Books

To learn more about rain, check out these Web sites:
http://www.nwf.org/nwf/kids/cool/water1.html

Index

Word Count: 80

Note to Librarians, Teachers, and Parents

PowerKids Readers (Nature Books) are specially designed to help emergent and beginning readers build their skills in reading for information. Simple vocabulary and concepts are paired with photographs of real kids in real-life situations or stunning, detailed images from the natural world around them. Readers will respond to written language by linking meaning with their own everyday experiences and observations. Sentences are short and simple, employing a basic vocabulary of sight words, as well as new words that describe objects or processes that take place in the natural world. Large type, clean design, and photographs corresponding directly to the text all help children to decipher meaning. Features such as a contents page, picture glossary, and index help children get the most out of PowerKids Readers. They also introduce children to the basic elements of a book, which they will encounter in their future reading experiences. Lists of related books and Web sites encourage kids to explore other sources and to continue the process of learning.